TAURUS HOROSCOPE
2015

Lisa Lazuli

Lisa Lazuli is the author of the amazon bestseller

HOROSCOPE 2014: ASTROLOGY and NUMEROLOGY
HOROSCOPES

ABOUT THE AUTHOR

Lisa Lazuli studied astrology with the Faculty of Astrological Studies in London.

She has practiced since 1999.

Lisa has been a regular guest on BBWM and BBC Shropshire talking about astrology and doing both horoscopes and live readings. She has also made guest appearances on Fox FM, BBC Cambridgeshire, BBC Northamptonshire, BBC Coventry and Warwickshire and US Internet Radio Shows including the Debra Clement Show.

Lisa wrote horoscopes for Asian Woman Magazine.

Now available:

TAURUS: Your Day, Your Decan, Your Sign

Includes 2015 Predictions.

The most REVEALING book on The Bull yet.

And

HOROSCOPE 2015 paperbacks for all the 12 signs.

Lisa Lazuli is also the author of

The mystery/thrillers:

A Sealed Fate

Holly Leaves

Next of Sin

As well as:

Delicious, Nutritious Recipes for the Time and Cash Strapped

Paleo Diet: Get Started, Get Motivated, Feel Great.

99 ACE Places to Promote Your Book

Pressure Cooking Reinvented.

Contents

FOREWARD

Dear Reader,

I hope my yearly horoscope for Taurus will provide you with some insightful guidance during what is a very tricky time astrologically speaking with the heavy planets i.e. Pluto and Uranus at loggerheads in cardinal signs, and Neptune in Pisces calling us all to get in touch with our spiritual side.

I have a conversational style of writing; please excuse any grammatical errors, I write much as I would speak.

As the song goes, "Nobody said it was easy." I know the mass media pump-out shows a plenty about quick fix love, money, fame and success; however, life is a journey filled with challenges and obstacles designed to encourage us to find out what we are made of, and who we really are.

Embrace the good and bad and enjoy what is your unique experience.

Be the hero in your own personal life movie and never hide your spotlight.

I must add that the best astrology insights are gained from a unique chart based on your time, date, year and place of birth.

If you would like your natal chart calculated for FREE:

Click here

http://lisalazuli.com/2014/06/30/would-you-like-to-know-where-all-your-planets-are-free-natal-chart/

Please join me on facebook:

https://www.facebook.com/pages/Lisa-Lazuli-Astrologer/192000594298158?ref=hl

It is time for a new level of intimacy and honesty with yourself. Taurus have reached a plateau in life: you can see clearly all around right now, and yet the landscape is empty, and it is up to you to shape that landscape and push on towards the horizon.

Taurus are feeling like it is finally OK to be who they are – you are accepting of yourself with all your quirks and unique qualities. You understand where you are in life, and while you may not be content right now, you are honest about where you are and how you got there.

It can be both very relaxing and also highly transformative to be in a state of mind of acceptance – from a position of denial, where can you really go but into more denial? When you are totally honest and true to yourself, you can be sure than any decision you make will be a reflection of the real you.

"It is what it is!" Yes, maybe, but nothing is constant, the world changes every day allowing us to change with it, and this year Taurus can mold their lives slowly and patiently just like a potter at the wheel with a lump of clay.

Superficiality is not an option this year; you need to explore more deeply who you are and what really makes you happy. It's easy to take a shop window approach to life, where you delude yourself that the lives and activities of others are glossy, fun and fulfilling while yours is not. You need to take serious stock of what is right with your life rather than thinking about what is wrong with it. Once you have given yourself a pep talk about all the positives, then you can begin to see how you can use those positives to change the negatives. You do not want to tackle the negatives head on as this may simultaneously put the positive in jeopardy.

2015 will have an element of "Phew; I made it." You have a strong sense of having got through a series of challenges, and you have taken quite a degree of self-confidence and pride from that, which has imbued you with a desire to take on more and press on further. Right now you have a definite sense of who you are and of your own personal power; it is time to cement that power by changing your world to reflect the inner sense of strength you have.

This is a year when if you apply a little effort, the results will be quite amazing – your spiritual will is in tune with your ego desires and that is why you can forge ahead without the usual barriers and hurdles. Even if you are passive, you can be presented with doors opening as it is that kind of year – somehow you are sending out all the right signals to the universe without doing any positive thinking.

Whatever you do, and whatever effort you put in it will be amplified due to the positivity surrounding you due to your chart configuration. You can be very effective when you deal with people due to your confident aura and the way you express yourself, being self-assured and commanding respect.

While this is not a year of drastic, turbulent changes, it is a year when you have the ability and inclination to make important adjustments to your life, which can make your life happier and more reflective of what your priorities are and what makes you fulfilled and happy. You know the saying, "Fix the roof when the sun is shining," – make this the year you tackle issues that are not going well before they become real problems. It is not only a time for fixing, but a time for improving – it is not always possible to mold your life the way you want to as some years are very turbulent, and it's enough to just keep head above water – that is why years like this are not a time to lean back, but to plan and execute on long terms goals and life improvements.

Use this year for pruning – getting rid of the dead wood and of the people and activities which you have grown out of and which no longer serve you. This is not a year of painfully extracting yourself from relationships, but rather letting go that which no longer plays a role in your life peacefully and harmoniously.

This a great time to get ahead and you may suddenly win a big contract or be given a role of far greater responsibility at work. Within business or government, you may be involved in reforms – you are the go-to person in all initiatives as you can get things done. You can deal with people in authority very effectively, which can be very handy.

This is quite a restless year for you: you need change and stimulation and may look to expand your circle of friends and look beyond your usual activities. You are more likely to plan weekends away and perhaps travel to visit friends and family more often than usual. You are looking to break up the routine and get inspired by doing a variety of activities and finding new pursuits.

A year of new friendships that will become strong and faithful ones.

It is an expansive year in terms of social life and your social networking. Within your work, you will have to be versatile and become an expert in many fields to increase your prospects and competitive advantage. Engaging directly with the public via Twitter, Google+, podcasts and webinars may be a new strategy that you employ to reach clients and communicate with potential customers. Traditional forms of media like radio and the print media may also play a role in your life, with you giving interviews or writing an article.

In 2015, you cannot get by, by ignoring change and doing things the old way – you have to update your skills and be on top of the latest trends in your industry. Legal changes and government law may affect the way you work, and perhaps you will have to restructure your business or retrain due to these changes.

This year will be one where you work hard and consistently. You are extremely determined and single-minded and have the clarity of thought and mental stamina to complete on long term and even complex projects. For Taureans who are studying, it may not all be plain sailing, and you may doubt your ability at times, but the message is clear, stick to what you are doing and so not give up. Doubts and hurdles can be overcome with consistent effort.

You are very inquisitive and will throw your efforts into learning anything that is new or involves current affairs and fast moving events; however, when you have to apply yourself to humdrum routine work and mundane financial matters, you will be really bored and find it hard not to procrastinate. So this is a great year for mental applied effort when it comes to new projects, but a great deal of willpower will be needed to complete the older projects or anything that you find tedious. I would devote the first part of the year to finishing and tying up old projects, get the boring jobs out the way as soon as possible so that you are freed up to take on more exciting and mentally liberating initiatives later in the year.

This is a very good year for Taureans trying to learn a new language or skill, and it is also positive for Bulls who are settling to a new country or career as you are more adaptable mentally and are excited by differences of any sort.

You cannot always rely on others for support and encouragement; this year you will look to yourself to draw the strength to thrive and survive. As the year goes on your self-belief will grow. It is a year of looking inwards for approval, not outwards. Whatever you do, do not go all out to be a people pleaser; there is a tendency this year to push the boat out to impress others and gain some sort of superficial reward or acclaim. The benefits of this are short-lived and rather hollow. When you are throwing your weight behind what you really believe in, you will have success and an inner warm glow – remember it is what you think of yourself and how you really feel about things that is important this year. Look within yourself for approval and support. You have great mental resilience and staying power; you have the thick skin needed and the determination to face anything and get through it.

It is a year of positive change when you are more in touch with yourself and thus able to make successful changes in line with your evolvement and growth. You have nerves of steel – I know you may not feel like that, but you are mentally stronger than you realize this year and can use that willpower and Taurean stubbornness to fight through any tough situation.

Taureans are never quitters, but this year you are more dogged than ever. You do not want to bang on relentlessly though as you can become very frustrated. Do not give up of course, but take breaks and mental breaks and learn to switch off mentally. You can grind down your competition this year with your incredible willpower and stickability.

There is a powerful drive to create more security in your life – financial security especially. You will also not stand for any bullying or being pushed about – you will stand firm on issues and not be coerced. It's a headstrong year, and you will have outbursts of temper when you feel that your identity or security (or that of your family) are threatened – you will make a powerful enemy.

This is a very sociable year, and single Taureans will meet and make many new friends with possible romantic encounters; however, it may not be a year for finding one stable partner to settle down with. Keep your options open and enjoy the dating and experimenting – remember this is a year to open yourself up to new experiences.

Relationships with men are far better than with women right now as it is men who seem to understand you. In intimate relationships you may be more reserved; it is important for you to have your own space.

Deep introspection and even self-examination can mark this year, in some ways it is a lonely year as you withdraw slightly from others. Although all Taureans will be highly sociable and have many group interactions, deeper and more meaningful liaisons with others may be few and far between. This is not a negative thing, but merely a reflection of your frame of mind and the considered, 'stand-back' perspective you are taking in your evaluation of your life. Taureans are more geared up for superficial and fun interaction socially; you are looking for distractions and are not really wanting or needing to share deeper feelings with friends.

On an intimate level, Taureans are enjoying good sex and their libido is high. Again, Taurus are emotionally dark horses as they keep their deepest feelings private even in close relationships and marriages. There is a time to share and a time not to share, and this year Taurus are not sharing and opening up. Your partner may be totally oblivious to this as your outer demeanor will give nothing away, and you will come across as rather jolly and fun-loving.

Relationships must evolve with you in order to survive long term as Taureans are undergoing a quiet internal revolution – amazing changes are happening which are leaving the Bull quite pleasantly surprised. Your perspective and understanding of your life is undergoing a profound change, and this is changing your outlook and the way you tackle problems.

A strong sense of realism and perspective will help you in all decisions and make this a very productive and fulfilling year.

You will think about things long and hard before you act, you will most likely delay making an important decision until the end of the month when you will act decisively and make an important choice which you will stand by.

You will not want to accept unfairness, either to yourself or towards someone that matters to you, and you will fight hard for a fair outcome. You may end up stirring up quite a hornets' nest in your quest for a just outcome, and the effects may create ripples far wider than you expected. Bear in mind before you embark on any mission/campaign or protest that there will be a backlash – make sure you are in a position to deal with it and that the end result will be worth it.

Beware of passive aggressive behavior from others, they may appear diplomatic and reasonable, but the aggression is concealed, and they may resort to sneaky and devious behavior to get their way without confrontation.

You are full of energy and enthusiasm and yet working in groups can be chaotic and frustrating with everyone pulling in different directions even though you are all committed to the goal. Avoid team efforts unless the roles you each play are well-defined, and the process is managed properly and not some ad hoc effort.

LOVE

Recently formed relationship may turn more serious this month, or maybe the things you are doing will be more mature i.e. meeting each other's families and spending time getting to know different generations of your new partner's family.

In marriages and long-term relationships, you will focus on practical matters that need to be ironed out for love to run more smoothly. You are very straightforward in love and will not have patience for games or complicated emotions. You are feeling rather sexual right now, be open and honest about that and make time for some fun with your partner. A nice evening out with some good food, then a nice drink to relax and some cuddles on the sofa and then some action. Make sure the kids are sent off to gran and that you have some extended time at home, so that nothing is rushed. This can be a very positive time both emotionally and sexually as long as you are not feeling pressured and are free to be spontaneous and express yourself.

Good sex this month may require some planning, but it is totally worth it.

Secure in yourself emotionally, this is a good time to take a relationship forward; if things have not been so good, this is the month to draw a line under it and move on positively.

CAREER

A good time to re-organize spending and arrange cutbacks in your outgoings or that of your business. A great month to prepare budgets and forecasts for your business as you are realistic but not overly pessimistic. Try and bring down accumulated debt starting from this month.

A grounded attitude will help you in all dealings and financial matters; like I said in the opening paragraph, big decisions will be delayed until the end of the month. You may feel that your hand is being forced in certain respects, but that may be a misconception, so do get good advice on important matters.

A fair amount of mixing business with pleasure and also socializing with business colleagues and clients. It is a time for cooperation and improving the way you communicate and cooperate with your business contacts becomes central.

Whatever industry you are in, it is time to be more creative in the way you work and how you present your business to others. A new marketing plan or advertising initiative can be very effective. As the focus is value for money this month, you do not want to spend heavily on marketing, the idea is to use your creativity and imagination to make a little go a long way when it comes to publicity. It may be a simple thing such as making your website look more attractive and accessible or a new set of business cards and a new logo. Think of how you project yourself and how your image can improve.

You are feeling quite restless this month and have an urge to stir things up and disrupt the status quo. It is unlike Taurus to be undiplomatic, but suddenly you feel as if there are things that should be said even at the risk of unpleasantness. You really do want to clear the air – this may have to do with events within your circle of friends or with a family member. It will be very hard for you to hold your tongue and even if what you say is not received well in the short run, you will feel much better for having raised it.

Taurus often err on the side of diplomacy and people pleasing to the point where there can be an imbalance in your life – your needs and feelings are often set aside for the sake of peace and quiet. Your over-arching need for harmony comes at a cost of bottling up – this month you will address that imbalance by skillfully communicating with others your feelings and grievances.

In some cases you may cut off communication with someone who has used you and taken advantage of your kindness and friendship – there has to be a line drawn at times, and this month Taurus must draw that line: firmly.

In career and home life, Taurus are finding their assertive side this month and so putting your foot down with people will come more naturally.

LOVE

Your assertiveness extends to romance, where you will find ways of ensuring your needs are met, and you are listened to. Relationships are not confrontational at all, but your partner will sense that you are bolder and no pushover. You are eager for sexual gratification and will take the lead when it comes to sexual advances and creating novelty in your sex life. Role play games may especially appeal to you.

Single Taureans may well make a move on an exciting new partner. Double dates, speed dating parties, are things you may consider as you look not only for relationships, but for new relationship experiences. Taureans are rather into looks this month – remember to give people a chance and not to be quick to judge.

A downside this month within all romances both new and old is the pursuit of perfection and perhaps unrealistic expectations. Yes, you are very giving in terms of love and affection, but you should not overreact if your partner does not give as much back – perhaps they have a lower sexual energy right now than you do. Try not to be too picky and specific about how dates should go, what you should do, how to get romantic – you may come across as controlling, and nothing is more of a dampener on romance.

Seek balance and harmony in your love life; do not let the physical become too much of a distraction, or you will lose out on true passion.

CAREER

A very good month for those who use language and words within their career – thus if you are a journalist, speech writer, politician, copywriter or writer of any kind you can have a real impact. Your words will flow, and you will have plenty of motivation to complete your tasks.

In most careers, expressing yourself will become more of an issue day to day, and you will have to use your communication skills. An ability to solve problems in your typically logical way will also come in very handy.

If you need to impress the boss or communicate with people in authority, this is a very good time to do it – you have an authoritative air about you, and people will take note and pay attention. Transits this month also favor teaching as you can hold people's attention and put things across well.

Working in a team or partnership can give you a big boost of energy and great confidence this month – you will achieve a lot and gain experience of authority.

Be assertive and bold in whatever you do, and believe in yourself and you will win respect this month.

Entrenched ideas and attitudes can cause you difficulty this month. You need to be more flexible in your thinking and more adaptable.

Many times in life we can cut ourselves off from what we do not want to accept or deal with – it can be a case of see no evil, hear no evil, etc. Of course, it is not in the nature of Taurus to change, and sometimes when confronted with a person or system with a difference in attitude it can be quite hard for the Bull to swallow. This month, you will be forced to deal with something you are not comfortable with. You may have to work in an environment or situation where you are really uncomfortable with the prevailing attitudes. You will be pushed beyond your comfort zone. Use this as a chance to re-examine your own attitudes and analyze why you feel this way. Is it your upbringing? Is it your innate nature? Is it conditioning? Is it fear? The answers to these questions could be very interesting and give you an insight into your own personality.

This is an opportunity to grow and be more open and accepting, in some cases your attitudes may soften, but this need not necessarily be true. The challenge is to be able to work with and get along with people whose views and values you oppose. You may learn to understand other attitudes more fully and thus be more comfortable with them. You may have to face the fact that these 'people' actually make you question your own beliefs, and that is why it is so uncomfortable.

LOVE

Changes your partner or spouse is going through may impact on the relationship this month. The health or family situation of your partner may cast a shadow this month and provide cause for more seriousness and attention to obligations.

Your partner is adjusting right now and may have their own issues to get through, which they cannot really talk about, and you need to be patient and supportive.

In new relationships, your partner's baggage may become a stumbling block to the relationship progressing forward. Unless there is a strong emotional bond and shared experiences, the gap in understanding can be impossible to bridge.

Sex life is inhibited due to outside pressure, but you should not allow this to become frostiness: affection, fondling, hugging and touching is essential.

Commitment is really tested this month, and you have an opportunity to show your partner that you are their rock, their confidante and the person they can always rely on.

The Taureans' desire to nurture and protect is brought to the fore in March. Perhaps in a karmic way of returning the favor.

CAREER

Trust and responsibility are important this month within your work. You may be entrusted with a large amount of money or be handed a very important client or contract. You will be handing something over which you must exercise extreme diligence and care.

You will have to exhibit leadership and show good judgment; you may be called to arbitrate a dispute, or you may have to make a decision which could impact on another person's reputation or future career prospects. This may put you in an uncomfortable position, and your ability to choose wisely and to be just and fair will be tested.

Fairness will be an issue in all your day-to-day decisions, and it will be hard to balance the needs and priorities of people and work. That is the challenge for you this month: to make tough choices with respect to the values and also financial implications for others.

Work will get busier as the month goes on with more interactions with clients and customers, you may travel to promote a product or sell to a new client.

You may need to take on board advice or input from various interest or action groups who lobby within your industry.

This month, things will seem to be going backwards: certain events and reactions of others may cause you to take a step back and reconsider.

It's a period when you will pause to take stock and perhaps re-think your strategy. Certainly not a month to push ahead regardless, you need to take some time to stop, listen, investigate and plan again.

This does not represent a major hitch at all, just a chance to re-adjust and rethink the way you are going about things. It can be really helpful to look at how you are feeling on an emotional and intuitive level about where you are at – this can help you take an insightful approach forward. This is not just about practicalities; it's about you. So much of this period (not only this year) of your life is about growth, personal power and achievement, what is going on internally is just as important as what is going on, on the outside. In a way, the external changes in your life are a mere reflection of the changes within you and so, problems that do arise should be analyzed in terms of your internal development.

You must feel 100% right about what you are doing, it must mean something, and it must contribute to your journey – whatever does not contribute must be dropped and your life may need some readjusting to get it 100% back on the right track.

By no mean a train crash; just a re-routing this month.

LOVE

Single Taureans can win over or impress a potential lover or new love interest this month by impressing them with wit, conversation, knowledge and skill. Show off what you know and show what a fascinating and well-informed person you are.

Take a fresh approach to looking for a partner by engaging in new social activities, including pub quizzes, charity runs, fetes, film clubs, etc. You are in a rather flirty mood and should have no shortage of potential partners to impress – that does not mean you will immediately settle for one, you may even keep a few on the go while you decide.

In marriages and permanent partnerships, you may annoy your partner by seeming erratic. You are in a playful mood and are not erratic at all, just restless and inclined to inject some much-needed fun and spontaneity into the relationship. This month you will do your best to avoid conflict and heavy emotional conversations, it's all about enjoyment and having fun again and rediscovering what it was like when your relationship was new.

Your partners need to respond to your need for fun and variety right now, as well as to your experimental needs. If he/she cannot respond, then he/she will have to give you some space so that you can fulfill these needs with your friends: not in terms of being unfaithful, but in terms of being with others who share your need for light-hearted, carefree fun.

CAREER

You may attend a course this month to improve your skills or to learn new ones. Versatility is essential within your job, and you must respond to changes quickly. You may be called on to devise plans and a new strategy for your team or department. There is a strong emphasis on adjustment and learning this month, with the necessity of quickly applying the new skills you learn in a practical way.

Within your business, you must focus on being more innovative in the way you process information and the way you communicate with clients. Think about how you can resolve client/customer problems quicker. How can you communicate about your new services and products with your clients/customers more effectively? Can you generate new ideas and products faster than the competition?

It is the month to be inventive and also very progressive in the way you communicate and interact at work with customers. Whether you run your own business or work for a boss, use your people skills this month to improve all aspects of customer relations and get a reputation for being a person who can deal with people and satisfy their needs quickly and efficiently.

The first part of this month is filled with positive energy, ideas and motivation. Your confidence will get a boost, and you will feel able to tackle things in terms of new initiative and projects.

It is ideal to pack in anything important before the 19th of May when Mercury turns retrograde: generally speaking, this is a time of confusion and misunderstandings, where plans to do with travel, contracts and communications can go haywire for no good reason.

You will tend to get quite a bit done before the 19th as you are inspired and more interested than usual, and your pace is really quick – you'll be amazed at how quickly things get done.

Post the 19th do take care not to overdo things and curb any tendency to exaggerate or promise more than you can deliver. Be careful post the 19th that you are not overcharged for anything; check carefully to see that what you do buy matches specifications.

Irritability and impatience can be a problem later in the month; try and remember how well the first part went, and remember that even if there are hitches after the 19th the average is still great.

LOVE

In relationships, you will not like to be put on the spot or coerced into making decisions you are not ready for. You can be rather evasive this month and will strongly resist being bossed around or controlled.

You are looking for growth and evolvement within the relationship, and where your partner is too set in his ways or too staid in his approach there will be problems. You are in a very outgoing phase of life where you welcome novelty; if your partner is happy to embrace this, then all the better for your relationship. If your partner is agro to your freedom loving, adventure seeking bent then you will drift apart (not necessarily permanently) this month. You are impatient with routine and with pettiness; you want to reject all those trivial aspects of day-to-day life and see a bigger, more promising picture. This is such a great year for Taureans moving forward, accepting that some problems cannot be solved, only outgrown, and the major stumbling block can be a partner who is still immersed in the very problems and trivialities you want to leave behind.

Another excellent month for single Taurus to experience new people for fun and love, but without the pressure of commitment.

CAREER

A great time to find new clients and customers and to sell more products or services. Also a favorable time to deal with legal issues.

The first part of the month especially is good for signing contracts, buying or selling, international trade as well as putting forward ideas and proposals. If you need to sell yourself i.e. at an audition or interview, any time before the middle of the month is great.

Travelling for business is also best done pre the 19th when Mercury turns retrograde.

Delay signing important documents after the 19th and do not make any strategic plans as you may make them in haste without the full facts.

You are adept at handling practical issues this month; however, you are far more focused on the big picture and smaller details are an annoyance. You will find multi-tasking frustrating as you will working with people. It is ideal for you to work at your own pace (which is quite fast) and alone this month. You are far more effective when working on a challenging project, anything mundane or meaningless will be a waste of the energy and ideas you have right now.

A burst of nervous energy, variety, surprises and people contact.

A month of information coming at you from all angles. Deciding what is important and what is not and how to prioritize can be quite stressful this month. There is so much going on at work, at home and in your social life, it can be both exciting and overtaxing, and you will have to do a juggling act.

This is a month when you can speak without thinking, and so do be careful of what you say as gossiping could leave you in an awkward position.

A good time to make amends if you have fallen out with a friend or colleague.

Be aware that as things are changing fast, what you felt or thought about something or someone two days back may not apply two days later. Remain flexible and delay in committing to anything hard and fast; you want to keep your options open.

If you are prepared to learn and accept some surprises, then this will be a very stimulating month. Let's be honest Taurus, last year you were bored, and this is just the sort of change and excitement you need to inspire you and help you get out of the ruts that had developed.

LOVE

There is an emphasis on entertaining in the home and on social gatherings with friends and family. You are feeling warm-hearted and generous right now, and that bodes well for sex and love in the relationship.

Taurus are highly passionate and amorous in the bedroom and will demand an equal response from their partners. Touching and physical intimacy, especially if it is spontaneous is what you are craving, and you will be happy to make the first move.

You are very giving emotionally and are happy to talk about your partner's problems and help soothe and inspire him/her. You are feeling great right now and have the extra positive energy and insight to give your loved ones to help them feel better too. Highly inclusive, you don't want anyone to feel left out or down, and you will do your best to bring out the fun and happiness in every situation.

The only downside in relationships is time: your partner may think he/she is last on the list. This is not true at all, but as with the opening paragraph, time is at a premium this month, so it's all about quality not quantity.

Single Taurus may have a sudden relationship with someone from a different culture or background – it could be a holiday romance but with a deeper level of understanding and friendship.

CAREER

There is an abundance of facts and figures to digest and mull over. You may also have to prepare reports in a short time and present findings. There is no time for detailed research, and you will have to get the gist of the information quickly and use it to the best of your ability.

Thinking on your feet and responding to changes and new info fast is what is required. You will have to manage your time very wisely and must quickly decide how the most productive way to use your time is – you cannot devote much time to projects or issues that do not deliver as this month it is all about the bottom line and keeping things moving.

Traveling within your locality to attend meetings or trade is a theme.

It will be very important for you to pick up information from your surroundings and use that immediately within your meetings or negotiations. Taurus are highly observant, and this skill will be very useful. You cannot really afford to turn off right now; you have to remain alert and anticipate responses so that you can be prepared.

A highly stimulating and interesting time when the learning curve will be quite steep, but your sense of achievement will be high.

You are in no short supply of energy and enthusiasm this month and what's more is that you are highly determined and willing to work hard. On the downside, you may overdo things.

Moderation is the key – do not force anything or anyone.

Physically you may be pushing yourself too hard. It may be that you are training for something in the sporting vein and are pushing your body to the limits – it is very important to recognize limits right now. Perhaps more can be achieved if you ease back on the pressure.

It is vital right now that you respect other people's limits as well, as part of the pressure you are putting yourself under may be directly impacting on someone you live with or work with, and you need to take their capabilities and feelings into account.

Too far too fast, is the pitfall this month. You have a certain air of invincibility which could lead you to over-extend yourself or miss certain warning signs. You need to be more aware of how what you do affects others; you could be accused of riding roughshod over others or of arrogance.

Ideally, you can achieve much this month and your positive drive attitude, when used to inspire and motivate others, can be very productive for everyone. However, if you act as if you are in a vacuum and are not responsive to the environment both social, political and emotional, you will waste time, energy and resources and not achieve much.

LOVE

Are you perhaps being too demanding this month? Is it all about you? A certain over-confidence could become overbearing and even bolshie, and this can really cause problems in relationships. Your opinions, work, ideas and needs may be overwhelming your partner; take a step back.

It may be hard for you to hold back this month in many respects, but if you can just focus on listening more and be more reactive to your partner, things will be far better.

The best use of the energies this month is if you and your partner can enjoy sporting or outdoor activities together – something that is energetic and consuming. There must, however, be give and take. Taureans are not in a very compromising mood right now: more stubborn than usual and stronger willed, you are not that easy to deal with.

I think that Taureans will totally underestimate how they are coming across – you are just full of energy and go, and this can be an advantage in relationships if you can work towards something meaningful for BOTH of you.

A passionate time in the bedroom, sexually a very good time.

CAREER

You are in a building phase of a new project now, and the difficulty is that some of the work you are doing feels as if it is at odds with the end goal. It can be hard to hold the vision while the groundwork is still ongoing – you must keep the faith in yourself and your goal. The long hours you put in now will begin to show dividends.

Yielding to the needs and wants of colleagues, co-workers or interests groups should not be seen as a sign of weakness, but rather as a secret weapon this month.

A good month to work on your public profile i.e. on LinkedIn or via business-to-business promotion.

Avoid reckless decisions taken in a moment of anger or frustration.

You may be headhunted this month – you never know where opportunities can arise.

This is a month of obstacle, hiccoughs and barriers to get through. Your strength, commitment and belief will be tested. You certainly can get over the hurdles, but it will be frustrating.

The transits this month often cause some pessimism. There is a fine line between realism and pessimism, sometimes they feel like the same thing, this month you are erring on the side of caution and that can be being a little pessimistic.

You will tend to doubt yourself, and you will push yourself to work harder and be more diligent and thorough to make up for that self-doubt.

Worry is also a feature of this month as you will tend to think more about problems, contingencies and money issues. This is not a bad thing as you are inspired to fix problems and perhaps think ahead to avoid problems. While this can be a time of negative thinking, it can be very useful and constructive if you can mitigate these potential problems with action.

Health-wise, overwork can cause some problems as you are run-down right now. You need lots of sunlight and exercise as well as fresh food. I would stay clear of extreme sports or excessive excursive as injuries to bones can sometimes result in this transit.

LOVE

A somewhat reserved approach can temper your love life this month. You are feeling drained both physically and emotionally, and you are not at your most open right now. You have withdrawn into yourself, and you are not able to really let your hair down right now. You will need to be a little quiet and have some time alone to think.

Lack of communication could be a problem if you do not explain yourself; be sure to make it clear to your partner that nothing is really wrong, you simply need some time. Often it is hard to be with others during a phase like this, you do not feel very sociable and constant thoughts of work, obligation and worry can cloud your social and free time.

Obligations in terms of the relationship may weigh heavy – you may have extra work due to issues with your partner's family, or folks or family problems may cast a shadow over life at home. Heated discussions about your finances or property are likely, and agreement on how to spend and where to save will be hard.

What you should not do is take any of this too seriously, it will pass, and the worst thing you can do is avoid the issues that arise. Tackle them systematically and patiently, and they will resolve.

New relationships may have difficulty this month, partly due to money issues and also due to different priorities and standards.

CAREER

It is time for a measured approach this month. The theme as you have read in the previous two sections is caution, slow and steady. You cannot push or force things this month, your freedom to act will be curtailed, and there will be times when you question yourself and wonder, "What next!"

You may have to deal with taxes, insurance, property and property taxes.

If you have been wasteful in terms of resources, now is the time to cut back and make up for that waste. Take a cautious approach in all money matters, especially where you hold money or resources jointly with another. This can be a very difficult month if you work with a partner as you may suffer as he may be ill or unable to work, or you may reach an impasse where getting agreement is impossible so work is held up.

You are quite a taskmaster this month and must be sure you do not expect too much of colleagues – you are not in the most understanding frame of mind, do try and be considerate.

You are very perfectionistic about work right now and can take on an immense amount of responsibility – with your willpower, persistence and determination, you will achieve far more than you actually thought you did this month.

Working through problems this month can really help you to be stronger and better equipped to deal with the rest of the year.

A far more optimistic month in September. This month can bring an abundance of new ideas and opportunities, but you must listen and be observant as there is much you can pick up. The pace of events will be quick, and you will be travelling and meeting many new people.

The first two weeks of the month are the best to make decisions as you are rational and unbiased and will perceive the true nature of any matter.

With Mercury turning retrograde square Pluto, mid-month your thoughts can become very intense, and you may over-think people or situations and become suspicious or paranoid about events. Sometimes you may be driven to extreme actions when under pressure.

You must look at things very critically this month, look for loopholes and catches. Be alert and pay attention to the nuances in people's behavior.

It is a nerve-wracking month, and you may find it hard to switch off. It is essential to take on an extra iron and Vitamin B complex with protein rich foods to support your nervous system. You must definitely devote time to anything that relaxes you, whether it be sport, music, movies, walking, etc.

LOVE

Relaxing is hard for you right now, and your fidgeting and inability to switch off may lead to accusations from your loved one that you are irritable and unresponsive to their needs. Taurus are highly charged at the moment, and you are not your usual easy-going self. You are prone to outbursts and may be accused of being a diva – it is not really that, it is more the fact that you are a little strung out and mentally overtaxed, so much so that you are tending to behave rather rashly

On the positive side, Taureans are very affectionate this month and generous in their emotions. What Taureans are not really geared up for in September is more serious and heavy discussions – if it's fun and lighthearted you are there in force, but you are inclined to set heavier issues to the side.

If your partner is in a positive, adventurous party mood then this month is perfect and will be great fun, filled with action and novelty. If your partner is not feeling as bubbly and outgoing as you then this may be rather difficult as you may see him/her as a wet blanket and so you may not have enough sympathy for his/her inner feelings.

While you are happy and loving in September, you are not necessarily patient or sympathetic; you do not want anyone raining on your parade.

Single Taureans may splash out and act extravagantly to impress. An excellent time to meet new people including love interests.

CAREER

As there is so much going on this month, there is a tendency to not be able to tell the wood for the trees in terms of arranging information and managing people. You can be quite overwhelmed by the pace of events.

Mid-month Mercury turns retrograde, and this is a time of intense mental concentration and requires the necessity to analyze and look deeper. What is required this month is getting rid of all the fluff and uncovering what really counts in terms of sales or your bottom line. You must strip out activities that are not essential. It will take time to find out which routes are the most effective as you will be bombarded with information and opportunities, but not all opportunities are worth pursuing, and you do not want to waste time on the marginally beneficial ones.

Political changes within your home country or a country with which you trade will impact on your business, allowing for some opportunities as well as adjustments that have to be made. Events will remind you this month that the world is still recovering from the financial collapse in 2008 and growth cannot be relied upon.

Attention turns inwards this month as you feel the need to turn the volume of everyday life off and listen to your inner voice.

Lately things have been such a whirlwind that you are wondering if you have lost some perspective. You may find yourself playing the role of confidante or advisor, and as you are in a transitory phase of life yourself, you will have a fair amount of support and advice to give.

This is also a time to pay more attention to your body's needs in terms of addressing diet and exercise, which you may have been neglecting or even perhaps overdoing – you need more balance and more moderation. It's been all work and all play, and this month you need to take stock and wind down mentally and physically. Get plenty of rest, fresh air and fresh food and quality sleep.

LOVE

Balance is also a theme in relationships.

Taking things personally and focusing on yourself instead of the partnership can cause some issues. You have the urge to fly off the handle over small things rather than, counting to ten and allowing the moment to pass – it is probably not worth making a fuss over after all. You are feeling quite self-conscious right now, and that may be at the root of you taking offence at small things. In new and older relationships, you must communicate with your loved one properly, do not assume anything, and do not assume that he/she knows how you feel, make it clear. Make sure all communication is two-way, it is not just about you explaining how you feel, it is also about you listening properly and understanding the way your partner feels.

You may need to discuss practical matters regarding how time each day is spent, the daily routines, chores and relative responsibilities.

Minor issues that niggle and grow into resentments need to be tackled now. Get on top of your bills – many arguments this month will be about money, so prepare a budget.

CAREER

You are very competitive and self-reliant this month and perhaps reluctant to work with others.

An excellent time for sorting out detail work. De-clutter your desk, get the office organized and pay more attention to fine-tuning the office procedures. Make sure the checks and balances you have in place work. This is also a time for communication with staff and colleagues about problems – get their feedback. Resolve any outstanding issues and try improve communication with clients and staff to prevent further problems.

This is a very good month for negotiating contacts – you are highly persuasive, and so you can be very effective as a negotiator or salesperson.

Within some careers, a great deal of bartering or legal jostling will occur this month – be ready to gather information, present it, defend it and sell it.

You are highly objective, logical and efficient this month and so work should be very productive, and you will see your skills, especially your writing and communication skills improving.

This is a very opportune month for those who work in sales, public relations, personnel, medicine, veterinary science or pharmaceuticals.

A feeling of well-being and optimism will carry you through this month despite some hard work and setbacks.

You are feeling very good about the way things are going right now, so much so that you will even be able to deal with problems and aggravating issues that arise with a smile. You're feeling quietly confident, and this will help you to grab opportunities and create a favorable impression on whoever you may want to impress.

What is really good about this month is that you have all the va va voom and confidence, and yet it is tempered by realism and the ability to foresee pitfalls and not drift into the unknown with rose-colored specs on. This is a good time to invest, purchase property or make long-term decisions.

Hard work at the start of the month will pay off, and you will see reward.

New ideas and visions of the future will begin this month, and you have the concentration to make some enquiries or do some very productive groundwork for these plans.

LOVE

The friendship side of your love relationships is very important this month. You will rediscover the strong emotional bond you have with your partner. There is a great deal of romance and a desire to be alone with your partner. It really is time to shut the world out and cozy up together.

Sex should be excellent this month as you are warm, sensual and very sensitive to your partner's needs. Poetry, movies, music all contribute to the very romantic and almost surreal love mode you are in now. The fantasy element of love-making is vital – it has to be an escape from reality and transcendence from the mundane.

Single Taurus may fall in love with a friend with whom you already share a bond. All relationships where you have a spiritual connection will thrive and grow this month as you seek to get in touch with your soul.

This is a month where the journey you are on as a human being really matters to you; meaning in life is what counts, and that is why all important relationships will get your full attention and appreciation. You want to immerse yourself in what really counts.

CAREER

I said at the beginning that this would be a year where you could really make changes and move forward as a person. You can feel the effects of that starting to pay off now, and you have the impetus to carry that forward to next year in an even bigger way.

You are already putting your vision for next year into planning mode. You are cautious and able to take well-considered risks. Disciplined and thoughtful, you are putting in excellent work right now, which may bring you to the attention of your boss – you may well be commended or promoted.

A mentor or someone in your company may take you under their wing and give you some excellent advice. If you are self-employed, you may look to someone you know, possibly someone retired who can offer you advice to give you the benefit of their experience. You are keen right now to get as much guidance as you can, and you are also keen to operate with social conscience.

You may find yourself more concerned about issues like being organic, environmental, fair and ethical trade considerations. Perhaps you will move to avoid suppliers that use child labor or who have poor working conditions.

You have a high regard for ethics within your workplace and are likely to report or perhaps reprimand colleagues or employees who behave in a negative, immoral or unethical way.

The pressure is off, and you can breathe a sigh of relief and enjoy the holidays.

This will be a very sentimental Christmas where you will seek to make a link to the past. You may perhaps remember or recreate a Christmas experience from your childhood or perhaps share with your partner or your children a Christmas experience from your past – something that means something to you.

There is an emphasis this holiday season on passing on something of lasting value i.e. family heirlooms, albums or even stories that can enrich the present with memories of those who may not still be with you.

You will spend much time looking back, reminiscing and taking stock, and this will not be a melancholy process, but one which is filled with warmth and perhaps a more positive fatalistic take on many of the things that have happened.

I see a mad rush after the 20th so try and get prepared early, there is more to do than you think, and you may have people arriving unexpectedly or get invites last minute. Make sure the tux and the sexy black number and red lippie are on ice ready to be hauled out at short notice.

LOVE

The sentimentality you feel this festive season will certainly inspire romance and love. Your partner may have thought you behaved like a Gemini most of the year, but you are back to the real you this December, appreciating home and all the simple and great things.

I can see you spending time preparing and wrapping highly personalized gifts. Taureans love to be creative, and at Christmas it is the most opportune time to be artistic by creating and choosing gifts that show your thoughtful and romantic side. Taureans are big old softies at heart, and you guys love to spoil – you far prefer the giving to receiving.

The sexual side of life is all about fantasy and escapism. Indulging romantic fantasies and creating some magic in your love life is very important. How do you do this? Surprising your partner, giving massages with exotic oils, some dressing up, making a show-stopping meal just for him/her or maybe (money permitting). You can travel possibly to a seaside resort, not necessarily a warm one, maybe to a log cabin by a frozen lake or a Norwegian Fjord or a chilly beach in Northumberland next to an ancient castle. Do something that inspires magic in the relationship – get away for maybe even two days to rebuild that spiritual connection you have with your loved one.

It will be easy for single Taureans to impress new and potential partners as you are so open and impressionable right now. You will get to know new people fast as you are very quick to share and relax with people you are meeting. Don't be a soft touch though – do not be too free and easy with everyone you meet over the holidays, some discernment and common sense must prevail.

CAREER

A very productive month for Taureans who work in music, the arts and spiritual fields. You will have quite a bit of work, and it can be financially and emotionally very rewarding work. You will have a fair degree of freedom to use your flair and imagination. You will strike the right notes in terms of your audience, and your performances will have more than the usual degree of impact.

The planetary aspects this month bode well for any seasonal activities, promotional or charity orientated that you may undertake as part of your business as long as they are highly creative and imaginative. Old ideas and last year's theme will just not hack it and so use your artistic side and go bananas.

The strong social conscience I spoke about last month is still much in evidence, and you may volunteer over the holidays or perhaps via your company donate or offer services to help a charitable cause.

You are in a very selfless giving mode and may also use your creative abilities to entertain or help others in some way.

You have drawn a great deal of strength and confidence in your abilities to succeed in your career this year – you should take some time to acknowledge all you have been through and the upheavals and challenges you have faced during the year. 2015 was not about the money; it was about you and finding a strength you thought you lost and rediscovering abilities and talents long forgotten.

CPSIA information can be obtained at www.ICGtesting.com
Printed in the USA
LVOW11s1450120115

422492LV00002B/335/P